Golf Clubs for Beginners

An Essential Guide to Understanding, Selecting, and Utilizing Your Clubs for Maximum Performance

Table of Contents

Introduction

For centuries, golf has been both a hobby and an exercise. It's a creative sport with elegant skill, precision, and strategy, and players take to the lawn to challenge their minds and bodies. Golf requires effort, skill, and quality equipment. A golf club is an important piece of equipment, a prized possession, and in this book, Golf Clubs for Beginners, you'll learn all you need to know about golf clubs.

If you're a novice and have yet to master the art of golf, this book offers a complete guide on golf clubs which will equip you with knowledge and information on the exciting world of golf by using step-by-step, easy-to-understand instructions.

Golf Clubs for Beginners delves into everything you need to know about golf clubs — how to pick them and how to use them. Using the right equipment is essential to grasp golf playing fully. In this book, you will be empowered with valuable insights, exposed to the different types of golf clubs, their purposes, and learn how they can help you to improve your performance. You will gain an understanding of the different types of golf clubs, and the book sheds light on details that'll broaden your horizons (and golf courses!).

You'll find information on maintaining your golf club and tips to improve your overall game. The book not only focuses on choosing golf clubs to suit your style but also looks at techniques to keep your golf clubs in top quality for a very long time. It goes over maintenance measures, ways to keep and store your golf clubs, and how to re-grip your clubs.

This book also contains information to guide you in developing your swing. With expert tips and advice, you'll learn the fundamentals to achieve a great swing, routines that fit in with your practice sessions, tips to enhance your swing, and how to achieve consistency.

Each chapter is a journey into a new dimension of golf clubs. You'll learn about club heads, shafts, and specialty clubs. You'll learn how to select clubs for different shots on different field pitches. You'll also learn how to select the best club heads for your shot and the common mistakes to avoid.

Golf Clubs for Beginners is an easy-to-read and practical book. It will serve as a guide to the challenging and equally rewarding golf methods. These pages contain the basics and secrets of golf clubs that you can use as beginners.

Grab your clubs and ready your mind as this book opens you up to the complexities and subtleties of golf. By the end of this book, you'll be well-versed in golf clubs, choosing the best club heads and maintaining them. You'll understand how to work on your swing, maintain consistency, and graduate from a novice to an experienced golfer.

Chapter 1: The Basics of Golf Club

When it comes to golf, there's a lot more to it than just hitting the ball into a hole. One aspect that often gets overlooked by beginners is the importance of understanding the equipment. Knowing about golf clubs, in particular, is paramount to anyone developing an interest in golf. This chapter will dive into the components of golf clubs, the different types of clubs, and why club fitting is so crucial. No matter where you are in your golfing career, understanding your golf clubs can be the make or break of your game. So, let's explore the art of the golf club!

What Is a Golf Club?

1. *Golf clubs are primarily designed to aid the player in hitting the golf ball with different degrees of lift and accuracy. Source: https://unsplash.com/photos/QZKFRL-HBUw*

When you hear the phrase "golf club," you may initially think of a social organization for golf enthusiasts. While that is a common meaning for the term, a golf club also refers to the tool used by golfers to hit the ball. Golf clubs are specialized sporting equipment used in the popular game of golf, which typically consist of a set of clubs of varying lengths and types. They are primarily designed to aid the player in hitting the golf ball, with varying degrees of lift, distance, and accuracy depending on the club's design.

The golf club consists of a grip, shaft, and club head. Each club head is uniquely designed and named based on its lift and purpose, ranging from drivers for long-distance shots to putters for short putts on the green. A golfer's choice of club greatly affects their shot accuracy and distance, making the selection of a golf club a vital part of the game.

Understanding Golf Club Components

Understanding golf club components is key to improving your game. As a beginner golfer, it can be overwhelming to understand all the distinct components that go into the design and construction of a golf club. However, gaining knowledge of these components can give you an advantage and help you make the right decisions when it comes to purchasing your clubs.

Grip

You need a comfortable and firm grip because it is the only point of contact between your hands and the club. You must select a grip that fits your playing style and hand size because grip sizes and types might vary.

Shaft

The long, thin piece that joins the grip to the club head is called the shaft. Steel, graphite, or a combination of the two materials can be used to create the shaft. Ball flight and shot accuracy are significantly influenced by the flexibility and stiffness of the shaft.

Hosel

This is the part of the club head that connects to the shaft. It plays a crucial role in the club's lift and angle, which determines ball trajectory and angle.

Club Head

This is the part of the club that basically makes contact with the ball. It comes in various shapes and sizes, and its design primarily affects the ball's flight distance, spin, and direction.

Face

The face is the club head's hitting surface and comes in a variety of materials, such as titanium or stainless steel. Whatever the material is, it generally affects the spin rate, launch angle and even the ball's speed.

Sole

The sole is the bottom of the club head and plays a role in the club's design and performance. Its shape, size, and weight distribution impact the club's turf interaction, ball flight, and spin rates.

Weighting

Weighting refers to the distribution of weight throughout the club head, shaft, or grip. Manipulating the weight distribution can influence the club's shot placement and shot distance. Understanding the different golf club components and their roles is necessary to improve your golf game.

Knowing what to look for in a club's grip, shaft, hosel, club head, face, sole, and weighting can help you find the perfect clubs or make the right adjustments to your current set. Investing in custom-fitting your clubs to your body type and swing style can also improve your game and help you reach your full golfing potential.

Types of Golf Clubs

Woods

The term "wood" in golf clubs originates from the historical use of wood to manufacture their club heads. While the heads of the contemporary woods are not made of wood anymore, the category name has remained due to their shape being similar to historical wooden clubs.

The woods are renowned for their larger club head sizes and have the longest shafts among all golf clubs. They usually feature hollow, round-shaped heads that extend a few inches from side-to-side and front-to-back, designed to provide a large surface of contact with the ball for longer shots with fewer mishits.

Within the wood category, the driver is the most important club and often the most significant investment for golfers. It is the longest club with the most oversized, bulging convex surface and is intended to hit the balls as far as possible. Golfers use the driver primarily from the teeing ground but can also use it on the fairway for long-distance shots. On the other hand, Fairway wood is a versatile type of wood suitable for different scenarios. Fairway woods usually have smaller head sizes than drivers, producing less distance but enhanced accuracy and versatility for various shots. Golfers often use fairway wood shafts for long-range — those ranging over 200 yards, or to navigate tight fairway spots.

Irons

Irons are a type of golf club typically used for shots that require precision and accuracy, such as those played from the fairway. They are distinguished from other types of clubs, such as woods and hybrids, by their smaller club heads and angled faces. The irons range from 3-iron to 9-iron or pitching wedge and are available in numbered sets. Each club has a progressively greater degree of lift and a shorter shaft length.

The construction of irons varies, with some featuring solid heads while others are hollow. The thickness of the club head is also much thinner than wood, earning irons the nickname "blades." Irons have slanted faces with grooves that are intended to grab the golf ball and add spin to keep it on the intended path. Using irons effectively requires skill and practice, as the short shafts and smaller club heads require a more precise swing than other types of clubs. When used correctly, however, irons are a powerful tool for golfers looking to improve their game, allowing them to achieve accurate shots and make their way around the course with greater finesse.

Hybrids

Hybrid golf clubs represent a revolutionary evolution in golf club design and technology. Combining the best attributes of woods and irons, hybrids are truly innovative and unique. A hybrid club uses materials and design elements from both wood and iron club types in the creation of its club head. A hybrid's primary function is to take the place of conventional long irons like the 2, 3, 4, or 5 irons.

For many golfers, these irons can be challenging to hit due to their smaller club head size, narrow sweet spot, and lack of forgiveness. Hybrids, on the other hand, offer a larger club head with a wider sweet spot, making it easier to hit consistent shots from a variety of lies, including rough, sand, and fairway. Additionally, hybrids frequently have a lower center of gravity than conventional irons, which aids in launching the ball higher and allowing it to travel farther with greater precision. The unique club head shape and sole design provide better turf interaction, allowing golfers to hit crisp shots from tough lies. Another great feature of hybrids is their versatility. They can be used for a range of shots, including tee shots, fairway shots, and approach shots from the rough or bunker. They are a flexible and useful club for golfers of all skill levels because they are efficient for chipping and pitching around the green as well.

Wedges

Wedges are a critical part of any golfer's club collection. These golf clubs have a distinctively angled club head, which sets them apart from other clubs and makes them ideal for hitting high-altitude shots with high accuracy. The steep incline of the club head enables golfers to achieve maximum lift and spin of the ball, thereby allowing them to land their shots softly and safely on the greens.

Wedge clubs are an essential component of a golfer's equipment, particularly when playing out of sand bunkers, chipping and pitching around greens, and hitting shorter approach shots into greens. They are widely used for these shots, as they offer a high level of control and precision that is necessary for these challenging golf shots. For instance, a sand wedge is extensively used to get out of a sand trap, thanks to its wide and heavily lofted club head.

There are several different kinds of wedges, such as the gap wedge, the pitching wedge, lob wedge, and sand wedge. Each of these has specific angles, loft, and bounce properties that make it ideal for different types of golf shots. The pitching wedge has a lower angle and is commonly used to hit shots between 100 to 120 yards. Meanwhile, the gap wedge is used for shots ranging from 90 to 110 yards, while the sand wedge is primarily designed for lofting the ball out of sand traps or hitting high-lofted shots around the greens. Lastly, the lob wedge is the most lofted wedge and is generally used for shots that require a short carry distance and a soft landing.

Putters

A putter is one of the most indispensable types of golf clubs used by players for putting on the green. The player rolls the ball into the hole with the fewest number of strokes possible using a putter club.

There are three different types of putters that players can choose from: the club head or traditional blade putter, heel-toe club head putter, and mallet club head putter. Among these different types, the most popular and traditional golf club is a club head or traditional blade putter. The club head putter is identified by its thin and flat blade and is widely recognized among golfers for its simplicity and accuracy while putting. Club head putters require the player to have a good degree of precision in striking the ball, as any slight misalignment can cause it to move off the target line.

Heel-toe club head putters are another variety of putters that have a slightly larger clubface and weight distributed toward their heel and toe. This type of club head putter has a larger sweet spot compared to its counterparts, which increases the chances of successful putts and reduces the tendency of off-center hits.

On the other hand, the mallet club head putter has a head that is circular or more significant, and it has a broad and flat front which helps the player to make more efficient and effective strokes, even from off-center positions. The heavier head of the mallet putter promotes a smooth, pendulum-like putting motion.

The Importance of Club Fitting

The club fitting process makes a significant difference in an individual's golf game. It is the process of customizing golf club components to fit the unique swing characteristics of the golfer. While some golfers neglect the importance of club fitting, it should be noted that getting the right set of clubs can be beneficial in many ways.

1. Improved Accuracy

A club fitting session is crucial because it helps golfers achieve greater accuracy. When the golfer is fitted with clubs of the right length, weight, and shaft flex, it allows for optimal swing mechanics, resulting in improved ball flight and accuracy.

2. Enhanced Distance

Club fitting ensures optimal launch and spin rates, which can add distance to a golfer's shots. Depending on the golfer's swing speed and launch characteristics, the club fitting can determine which club head and shaft combination will give the highest ball velocity and carry distance.

3. Better Consistency

Having inconsistently fitted golf clubs can lead to inconsistency in your golf shots. Custom-fitted clubs help golfers maintain a more compatible swing, creating a more controlled ball flight for more predictable results and a better overall experience on the course.

4. Improved Comfort

Custom-fitted clubs are designed specifically for the golfer's body and swing characteristics. This creates an improved level of comfort and confidence on the course, which ultimately leads to more successful shots.

5. Minimized Risk of Injury

A well-fitted club reduces the risk of injury by creating a more efficient swing motion. Improper grip size can cause pain and discomfort, leading to injuries to the hand, wrist, and elbow. A club fitting session can ensure that the grip size, shaft length, and weight are all optimized to reduce the risk of injury and pain.

6. Better Long-Term Results

Club fitting helps golfers play better and reduce their handicaps. It helps determine a player's strengths and weaknesses and recognizes the best clubs for their style of play. By creating a more efficient swing motion and addressing any discrepancies in the player's stance, club fitting can establish a solid foundation for long-term improvements in their game.

7. Return on Investment

Spending money on custom club fitting can be considered an investment in your golf game. A well-fitted set of clubs will not only enhance your performance and improve your consistency but will also last longer, ultimately saving you money in the long run.

Chapter 2: Drivers and Woods

2. *Golf drivers are often made from lightweight materials to allow for optimal swing speed and power. Source: https://unsplash.com/photos/_-6iQvIunqA*

Golf drivers are clubs designed to hit the ball the furthest distance and allow golfers to achieve long shots down the fairway. Drivers are considered the fundamental and most necessary club type in a golfer's kit. They are often made from lightweight materials such as titanium, graphite, or carbon fiber to allow for optimal swing speed and power.

Drivers are used on the first shot off the tee because the player needs to hit the ball a long distance right away. They are made expressly to deliver the most distance for golfers targeting a long drive on the tee box. The clubface on a driver is often much larger than other club types and has a greater degree of lift. The angle of the clubface at impact with the ball creates an optimal ball flight that can travel significant distances with minimum spin and as much accuracy as possible.

Different driver styles are available on the market from various manufacturers, each offering unique characteristics, features, and benefits. Here is a detailed overview of different types of drivers in golf.

Standard Driver

A standard driver is the club type that makes up a large percentage of the driver's market. It is the most commonly utilized driver by many players, regardless of skill level. Standard drivers have a considerable head size and a broad sweet spot. They often come equipped with an adjustable weighting system, different lift degrees, and lengths to personalize your golf club to suit your preferences.

Offset Driver

An offset driver is a driver with a clubface that is set back from the shaft. This type of driver is similar to a standard driver in that it is designed for off-the-tee play. The offset driver's main advantage is that it corrects a golfer's slice or push shots by promoting a draw or hook spin to the ball. It can position a player's hands slightly ahead of the clubface, resulting in a different angle of attack, which can also improve ball flight.

Adjustable Driver

An adjustable driver is a club where the player can modify several characteristics based on personal preferences. From adjusting the lift and center of gravity to weight distribution, drivers with adjustable weights and hosels allow the player to alter their club to their unique swing.

High Loft Driver

A high loft driver is a club that elevates the ball higher in the air but with less distance off the tee. It is frequently used by seniors, women, and beginners who have difficulty achieving the swing speed to take full advantage of a standard driver. They often have a fixed loft between 14 and 16 degrees, ensuring the ball is often sent on a higher trajectory, which is necessary for golfers with slower swings.

Low Spin Driver

Low spin drivers decrease the spin generated on the golf ball by a lower swing speed player. They benefit players who struggle to find fairways on their tee shots. The low spin driver features a lower profile head with a smaller circumference clubface to assist in the launch and reduce drag that often causes unnecessary spin on the ball.

Draw-Biased Driver

A draw-biased driver is intended to help a player produce a draw shot or counter the effect of a slice. It can provide more control and confidence while off the tee, making it an excellent option for golf beginners. The club face on the driver offers a closed face angle, club head weighting, and, at times, an offset hosel that helps the player square up the club face.

Characteristics and Features of Drivers

Accuracy

One of the most important characteristics of a driver in golf is accuracy. This refers to the ability to hit the ball with precision and control, sending it exactly where the player wants it to go. With a driver, players aim to hit the ball straight and far down the fairway toward the green.

Loft Angle

A driver's loft angle refers to the angle between the clubface and the ground. Most drivers come with a loft angle between 8 and 13 degrees, depending on the player's skill level and swing speed. A low loft angle is best for golfers who desire more roll on the ball and have a faster swing speed, while a high loft angle aids in launching the ball higher.

Club Head Size

Another key feature of golf drivers is the club head size. In a golfer's set, drivers typically feature the largest club heads, allowing for the largest sweet spot. Players can hit the ball more consistently and even on off-center hits thanks to a wider sweet spot.

Shaft Length

A driver's shaft length can significantly impact swing speed and distance. Drivers generally have longer shafts than other clubs to allow greater acceleration and more speed through impact. However, longer shafts can be difficult to control, particularly for beginners or players with slower swings.

Adjustable Features

Some modern drivers come with adjustable features such as loft, lie angle, and center of gravity. These adjustable features allow players to personalize their driver for their own style of play and swing mechanics. For example, you can adjust a driver's loft angle to launch the ball higher or lower depending on the course conditions and your swing speed.

Forgiveness

Many golfers rightly take into account a driver's forgiveness. This refers to the club's ability to reduce the impact of off-center hits and other mishits, making them more forgiving. Forgiveness is particularly helpful for beginners or players who struggle with consistency as it increases their chances of enjoying the fun of the game by avoiding frustration on the course.

Shaft Flexibility

This directly impacts the swing speed, ball compression, and launch angle. There are five different flex levels for drivers: super stiff, stiff, ordinary, senior, and ladies. For golfers with faster swing speeds, a stiffer flex results in less shaft bending throughout the swing, which improves control and accuracy.

Club Head Volume

The size of the club head plays a role in determining your golfing success. The maximum legal club head volume, per the United States Golf Association (USGA) rules, is 460cc. A larger club head volume leads to a larger sweet spot, which makes it easier to hit the ball straight and far, even on off-center shots.

Weight Distribution

A driver's weight distribution is designed to lower the center of gravity for better ball flight, accuracy, and distance. Drivers who lean heavily towards the toe encourage a fade ball flight, while those who lean heavily towards the heel promote a draw ball flight, while those

Material

Drivers are made from different materials, such as titanium, carbon fiber, or steel. Titanium is a highly sought-after choice due to its lightweight yet strong qualities, allowing more weight to be redistributed toward the perimeter of the club head for increased forgiveness and stability. Carbon fiber is another popular material for drivers due to its lightweight yet durable properties. Choosing the right material is down to players' preferences.

How to Select the Right Driver for Your Game

Selecting the right driver for your golf game is a crucial step toward achieving success on the course. You can improve your shot accuracy and distance by selecting a driver that suits your abilities. Here's how you can select the right driver for your golf game in 5 easy steps:

1. Determine Your Swing Speed

Your swing speed plays a critical role in selecting the correct flex for your driver. You can determine your swing speed by visiting a local golf pro or by using a launch monitor to get an accurate reading.

2. Assess Your Skill Level

It's essential to assess your skill level before purchasing a driver. If you are a beginner or an intermediate player, opting for a driver with a larger sweet spot for increased forgiveness is better. An advanced player may prefer a lower lofted driver for added distance and ball control.

3. Choose the Loft

The loft of your driver affects the trajectory of your shot. A higher lofted driver is typically suitable for those with a slower swing speed. Advanced players who have a fast swing-speed and require added control prefer a lower lofted driver.

4. Select the Shaft Material

The material of your driver impacts your swing speed, accuracy, and distance. Graphite shafts are lighter and more comfortable to handle but may cost more. A steel shaft, however, can be more durable and provide added control.

5. Test the Driver

You must always test the driver before making the final purchase. Try the driver on the course or visit a golf store where you can hit some shots into a simulator. This will help you determine if the driver is the right fit for your game.

Fairway Woods

Fairway Woods are the most versatile clubs in the game of golf. They are designed to be used when hitting from the fairway, hence the name fairway wood. Typically, golfers will carry a three-wood and a five-wood in their bag. These clubs are used to hit longer shots than irons but with more accuracy and control than drivers.

Fairway woods are forgiving, making them easier to hit than drivers. They have larger club heads than irons, which gives golfers a larger sweet spot. A larger sweet spot will make you less likely to mishit the ball.

The three-wood is designed to hit shots between 200 and 240 yards. It is used off the tee on shorter par-4s or on long par-3s. The five-wood can hit shots between 180 and 220 yards and is primarily used on longer par-4s or on shorter par-5s when the golfer wants to lay up instead of going for the green in two shots.

Fairway Woods are also great for hitting shots out of the rough. They have a low profile, so they can slide under the grass more easily than irons. Fairway woods also have a lower center of gravity than irons because to the weight distribution, which makes it simpler to move the ball up in the air and out of the rough.

In addition to hitting shots out of the fairway and rough, fairway woods can also be used to hit shots from the tee. Some golfers prefer to stick to their three-wood off the tee on shorter holes because it is more accurate than their driver. Some golfers find that they are more consistent with their fairway woods than their drivers.

Fairway woods are versatile clubs that can be used from the fairway, rough, or tee. They are forgiving and offer golfers more control and accuracy than drivers while still allowing them to hit longer shots than irons. If you're looking to improve your game, consider adding some fairway woods to your bag.

Chapter 3: Irons and Hybrids

3. Irons have smaller club heads and shorter shafts, and help golfers make accurate holes. Source: https://unsplash.com/photos/biDxI-pL25g

Equipment facilitates performance, which is crucial to a player's success in a particular sport. In golf, an iron is one piece of equipment that helps golfers make accurate holes. It determines the success or failure of a hole. Usually made of steel or solid iron, irons have smaller club heads and shorter shafts. Irons play a fundamental role in golf, making it easier to strike the ball over a long distance, add spin, and hold the golf club. Among golf clubs, irons are the most common. A standard golf club set contains 7-11 irons, including wedges. These different types make up a typical, traditional golf set, and golfers divide them into three groups, namely the short, mid, and long irons. They are categorized in descending order — the long irons cover from 1 to 4, the mid irons from 5 to 7, and the short irons are from 8 and 9, plus the wedges.

The Varieties of Iron

The different irons in a golf set are used to hit the ball on different parts of the pitch and to different distances. These irons have distinct shafts and lofts, which adds to the reason for their specific use. The many varieties of iron are categorized into short, mid, and long irons.

Long Irons

The driving iron is the first iron and falls within the category of long irons. They have a long shaft and a really low loft, contributing to the distance the ball will cover.

Mid Irons

Mid irons provide room for error due to their significantly shorter shaft. They're also regarded as utility clubs due to their greater loft, which gives them a greater surface area. They have more spin and a higher trajectory.

Short Irons

The 8 and 9 irons are classified as short irons. Among them are the pitching wedges. As their name suggests, they're the shortest of all the clubs. They are useful when making shorter shots because they have the largest club head mass and shortest shafts.

Golf irons come in two designs: the cavity back and the muscle back irons. The cavity back irons were initially designed for average golfers and beginners, despite recent growth in its popularity among professional players. They are made to have a larger sweet spot, which makes it simpler to make a straight shot and gives the ball some elevation. Muscle back irons, sometimes known as blades, are intended for experienced players. They have a small sweet spot and thin top line that make it simpler for players to shape the ball. The player's iron is made for low handicap golfers and professionals to ensure that the ball travels farther, while the game improvement irons can also be helpful for amateurs and golfers with high handicaps. These various irons help players achieve maximum forgiveness and high launch. Players with a moderate swing speed are mostly accustomed to this set of irons.

These irons are excellent for a regular golfer. They can help you hit specific distances, accurately make shots and record a high success rate when attempting holes.

Choosing the Right Iron for Your Swing

Choosing a set of golf irons to give you the right blend of distance, feel, and flight can be difficult. You want a set of irons tailored to your style, which still gives you the confidence and accuracy you need to make your shots. There are a couple of factors to consider before making your final decision on the irons that make up your golf set. These include:

1. Determine the Iron Type

When choosing a golf iron, select the one that suits your game. Select an iron that gives you a seamless blend of ball striking and playing ability to achieve ideal performance. There are many types of golf irons shaped in different styles, but choosing the one your favorite golfer uses doesn't guarantee you'll perform at that level. You'll need a golf iron that suits your skill level. It helps to combine different brands to create a combination set but remember to choose one that fits your style and allows you to perform to the best of your ability.

2. Consider Your Budget

Your budget is one of the most defining factors when choosing a golf iron. The pricing for irons ranges, and it increases with the quality. Your budget determines what type of iron you buy, but you don't have to break the bank to get quality irons. You can also buy second-hand products, which will be less costly, but you must be careful and avoid common pitfalls. You can also invest in head covers to keep your iron heads pristine for longer.

3. Get Custom Fits

If you're attempting to get an iron for your swing, you'll want one that fits just right. Custom fitting helps you fully utilize your iron. However, bear in mind that they can be very expensive. Custom fitting ensures that your irons are suited to your playing style — how you deliver the ball, your swing speed, and your height. You'll use golf irons for every hole, so get one that matches your playability.

4. Test Different Heads and Shafts

You'll never know the right fit unless you try them out. Test out the heads before choosing the iron that goes in your set. Try as many as possible until you're satisfied. It'll be worth your while, and once you've found the head that can improve your game, try different shafts. No one size fits all, and the old eye test doesn't help select the best iron.

Picking the iron that suits your swing isn't hard if you consider the right factors and your abilities. Take your budget into account, along with the different heads and shafts, and always read reviews. Research credible information about the product and brand before buying to ensure you're buying appropriate gear.

Hybrid Clubs

Hybrid clubs are becoming increasingly popular among players and have begun to phase out the cavity back irons. Hybrids are a mixture of irons and woods — similar to wood in volume yet similar to iron in club head, material, and length. Their main characteristics include a low profile and center of gravity, hollow club head, offset, improved loft, and use of different metals. They are easier to handle and swing and provide better accuracy when moving the ball in a certain direction. They're perfect for both beginners and experienced players.

Advantages and Disadvantages of Hybrids

Hybrids were originally designed to help golfers get out of the rough and add a lot of flight to the ball. Over time, companies have made hybrids feel and look great. They're an impressive choice for all levels of handicaps. However, there are some advantages and disadvantages worth noting.

Advantages

- More appealing head design

- Easier to hit

- Allows for more consistency

- Allow for more game confidence

- Improved launch trajectory

- Useful to get out of the rough

Disadvantages

- Doesn't improve everyone's game

- Better suited for novices and high handicaps rather than pros

- Less feel and control compared to irons

- Takes more time and effort

Golf clubs assist in performance and taking shots. Whether you choose an iron or a hybrid, adequate information about the equipment will help you acquire a good fit. With this knowledge, you'll achieve a better trajectory, spin, and launch on the ball. Be diligent and test out your options to choose an iron that matches your swing.

Chapter 4: Wedges and Specialty Clubs

4. *Specialty clubs help make strokes more precise and are used on the putting greens, for the last strokes played on a golf hole. Source: https://www.pexels.com/photo/a-golfer-in-driving-range-4954265/*

As a beginner golfer, you will improve your skill by identifying and understanding the standard equipment through practice and getting comfortable using the items. Your golf bag is packed with different clubs for a reason, and knowing whether to use a wedge from the iron set or a specialty wedge can be challenging. Understanding their different roles will have you make good decisions on the course. This chapter is a complete guide on the roles of various wedges and their uses in golf. You will also learn about specialty clubs like putters, chippers, bump and run, and their uses to expand your knowledge.

The Role of Wedges in Your Golf Game

Wedges are the primary-lofted clubs among golf clubs made for short distant shots. For most golfers, it could be 120 yards. Wedges were also designed for shots from sand, pitch shots, and chip shots. The role of golf wedges is to hit the ball high up or to come down quickly using a high amount of spin. Golfers use wedges for different reasons, like clearing a rough area, leaving the bunker, or hitting any difficult shot.

Different Types of Wedges and Their Uses

Although golf wedges are present in different loft angles of 45° to 60°, the four standard wedges are sand wedges, lob wedges, pitching wedges, and gap wedges.

Lob Wedges

Lob wedges are sometimes considered extreme, with a normal fall range of 58° to 64°. A lob wedge with a minimum amount of roll can produce a short angle of ascension and descension. A lob wedge IS your ideal wedge club for hitting a flop shot, chipping from tightened lies, hitting shots all over the green, or any other variation of shots where you want the ball to be high and have a soft landing.

Sand Wedges

Sand wedges were designed to get your golf ball away from sand bunkers. It has a greater loft of 54° to 58°. The higher loft of a sand wedge serves as a shovel for getting the golf balls out of the sand trap. A sand wedge can be used for full-swing shots, bunker shots, pitching all over the green, flop shots, and half-swing shots.

Gap Wedges

Gap wedges are majorly designed for shots unsuitable for a pitching wedge or sand wedge and, as such, lie in the middle. A gap wedge is a multipurpose wedge used for shots like half-swing shots, complete shots, and chip and run shots at the higher end of the loft.

Pitching Wedge

A pitching wedge has a loft angle of 44 to 49° and is used for a shot of approximately 100 yards in magnitude. As with sand wedges, the pitching wedge is named based on its pitching ability. A pitching wedge is ideal for beginner golfers and can be used for complete-swing shots, chip and run shots, chipping and pitching shots, and punch shots.

Specialty Clubs: Putters, Chipper, and Bump and Run

You may be missing a couple of specialized clubs from your set that could help take your game to the next level. You may have been playing for a while using clubs from your beginner's bag and now notice some missing pieces in your collection. It shows you're advancing your skill. Hence, it's time to upgrade your golfing arsenal. Below are some specialized clubs that will boost your game.

Putters

Apart from a putter being one of the finest specialized golf clubs, it comes in different sizes and shapes. Golfers use it to put the ball into the hole on the putting green. Compared to other golf clubs, putters come in a variety on the market. This could be a result of individual preferences of putters. There are no right or wrong putters. Your choice of putters is based on what works for you. Putters come in three club heads and three arrays of length. Note the following on putters:

Club Heads

This can either be a heel-toe club head, a mallet club head, or a traditional blade. A normal blade is compact and shallow, with the shaft at its heel. Aside from the additional weight at the heel and toe to provide a weighting perimeter, the heel-toe has the same shape as the normal blade. Furthermore, it has other designs to make the club more lenient on botch hits. The club head-on mallet putters are large, which enables them to take advantage of poor contact with the ball. Mallets also come in a variety of shapes and sizes and shapes.

Personality

The idea behind using putters is reliant on personal preference. Putters are only as efficient as the person is comfortable using them. The workings of putters all come down to your confidence — do you feel comfortable wielding the putter? Does it feel natural? If your answer is yes, then you've found your match.

Length

Conventional putters are also standard lengths ranging from 32 to 36 inches at both ends. They are well known for their length, which is the ideal size recommended for beginners.

The grip of the belly putter's end comes up to the golfer's belly because of its length. On the other hand, the broomstick putter's upper range is 40 inches, and the lower range is 50 inches causing the gofer to stand vertically. Despite the variations in their size and shape, putters are designed to let the golf ball roll more easily and with less backspin in order to prevent skidding. Most putters on the market today have a 3° to 4° amount of loft.

The Chipper

The Chipper is a well-known specialty club often seen in local or commercial professional shops. The chipper looks like a putter due to its low lofted wedge design. It was made to provide natural chip and run shots between 30 to 40 yards, giving the golfer room to make putting shots.

What makes the chipper stand out is its degree of loft, which is about 38 to 39, the same as a 9 iron, and it has a length of around 35 inches.

A chipper, just like a 9 iron, can get you closer to the ball. With it, you can have more regular short games and make real contact with the ball.

The chipper clubs perform better in some situations, such as when you hit a chip within the 40-yard range with no barriers ahead. You are to use this club only when you are close to the putting green with no ponds, bunkers, or rough in your way — when you hit the ball, it has no spin, and if there is any barrier in front of it, it will not be able to go over it.

The Bump and Run

"Bump and run" is golf terminology for a unique type of shot. It is regarded as a chip shot not often used by golfers. Whenever you decide to play bump and run shots, the focus should be ensuring that the ball is low, then you hit it like a bump allowing the ball to run into the putting green close to the golf hole. Golfers tend to use a short-range iron when using a bump-and-run club to hit a shot. These irons could be seven or eight coupled with a pitching wedge. These clubs are efficient due to their loft as it keeps the ball grounded enough to manage its speed and steer clear of any obstacles. The ball should be proportionately high to control where and how it lands. Some golfers use three pieces of wood to indicate when it is close to the green. It is sometimes a tough call to make, so golfers rarely use it.

The golfing club you choose affects how you play the game, so make sure you feel confident with one in your hands. Keep in mind that practice makes perfect — the more you practice, the better you'll play.

Chapter 5: Understanding Shaft Types and Flex

For every club you pick, you need a perfect matching shaft to go with it. The shaft is the key aspect of any golf club; it controls your accuracy, distance, and the overall feel of each shot. So, if you've been struggling with inconsistent shots or want to gain a competitive edge, understanding shaft types and flexes is necessary. In this chapter, you'll learn the importance of shafts, the different shaft materials, and how to determine the right amount of flex for your unique swing.

The Importance of Shafts in Golf Clubs

Shaft Length Comparison

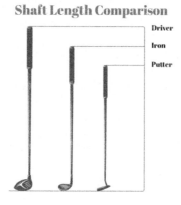

Driver

Iron

Putter

Shafts are important in the game of golf for the following reasons:

- Shafts in a golf club are just as important as the club head. The Shaft is the conduit between your hands and the club head, so you'll want to choose one that suits your swing.

- Shaft material affects a club's flexibility, weight, and feel. Steel shafts are inexpensive, durable, and consistent but can feel stiff. Graphite shafts are lighter, more flexible, and absorb vibration better.

- The shaft is a crucial element of your golf clubs, so take the time to understand how different materials and flexes work with your unique swing. When you match the right shafts to your game, you'll gain power, precision, and consistency—and your performance will improve.

- Shaft flex refers to how much the shaft bends during your swing. If your shaft is very stiff, you'll lose accuracy and power. Too much flex reduces control and consistency. For most casual golf players, a regular or senior flex shaft works well.

To determine your shaft flex, pay attention to your swing speed and ball flight:

Swing Speed

Use a launch monitor to measure your driver's speed in miles per hour. Below 85 mph needs a senior or ladies' flex; 85-95 mph uses regular; 95-105 mph uses stiff; over 105 mph needs more stiff flex.

Ball Flight

If your shots go left, you may need a stiffer flex. Shots that go right often indicate too much flex. A balanced, straight ball flight means using the right flex for your swing.

Different Types of Shaft Materials

You must factor in their material and flex when it comes to shafts.

Shaft Materials

1. Steel Shafts

These are generally inexpensive, or rather less expensive, when compared to graphite shafts, but they can be heavy and difficult to control. These shafts are also stronger and considered more durable than other types of shafts. This is a good choice for beginners because they reduce the feel and add weight.

There are two types of the steel shaft:

- Stepped steel shaft
- Rifle steel shaft

2. Graphite Shafts

These shafts are lightweight, absorb shock better, and allow for more flex options. For this reason, they are a popular choice among female and older golfers. The lightweight nature of the hold gives it the added ability to produce better swing speeds, but it also means that with the amount of flex the swing generates, control is nearly lost.

3. Composite Shafts

This type of shaft is also called a multi-purpose shaft. It combines steel material and graphite, creating a material that balances weight, power, and price. The composite shaft is an all-purpose shaft.

4. Titanium Shafts

This shaft material is relatively new in the market. Titanium tends towards the stiff side, making it strong. They are lighter than steel but stronger than graphite. These types of shafts can dampen vibrations, making them ideal for strong golfers who encounter some hassle getting the needed distance on their shots. However, they may have accuracy to worry about with this type of Shaft.

Shaft Flex

Your golf shaft's flex refers to how flexible or stiff it is. It significantly impacts how much the shaft bends when swinging. Stiffer shafts bend less, while more flexible shafts bend more. The right flex for you depends on the speed of your swing and also your distance.

Swing Speed

1. **Slow Swing (80 mph or less):** Slow swings require more flexible shafts (A or L flex). To achieve this, go for a lady's or senior flex shaft. Flexible shafts are designed for slower swing speeds, giving you the most whip through the ball. A too-stiff shaft won't load and release properly, resulting in little power or control.

2. **Moderate Swing (80 to 95 mph):** A regular or average flex is ideal for a moderate swing. It

balances control and power for most recreational golfers. A regular flex shaft will bend moderately but stabilize well at impact for solid, consistent shots.

3. **Fast Swing (95 mph or higher):** Fast swings require a stiff or extra-stiff flex. They need stiffer shafts (S or X flex) than the slow or moderate shafts to produce solid shots. If a shaft is too stiff, you'll lose accuracy and distance. If it's too flexible, you'll lose power and control. Those who are starting out would do well with a regular or senior flex (R or A flex) graphite shaft, and as their swing develops, they could move into stiffer flexes. The only way to know for sure is by getting fitted by a pro, but understanding the basics about shafts and flex will help you make an educated choice.

With the variety of high-quality shafts available today at different prices, you're sure to find one that suits your swing and helps you get the most out of your game. Moreover, the flex for your irons and wedges should be one level softer than your driver. So, if you have a stiff driver shaft, opt for a regular flex in your irons. Keep practicing and focus on consistent contact — those low scores will be just around the bend!

Tempo

Your swing tempo also impacts which flex will work best. A faster tempo means transitioning quickly from backswing to downswing, requiring a stiffer shaft. A slower tempo with a pause at the top needs more flex.

As a general rule:

- **Fast Tempo**: Use a stiffer flex

- **Moderate Tempo:** Use the recommended flex for your swing speed

- **Slower Tempo**: Choose a softer flex

Shaft Flex: Finding the Right Match for Your Swing

Choosing the right flex for your swing speed and style is key to maximizing your performance. Take the following considerations seriously to help simplify your choice:

- **If you have a powerful, aggressive swing, you need a stiffer shaft** that won't bend excessively. Shafts that are too flexible won't stabilize at impact, leading to wild, uncontrolled shots. A stiff or extra-stiff flex will load and release precisely to maximize your power and accuracy.

- **Test different flexes to find your match**. The only way to know how a shaft will perform is to test it in person. Most shops offer shaft testing and fitting to determine which flex and overall shaft will complement your swing best.

- **Consider your tempo and release**. Faster tempos and later releases often require stiffer shafts, while slower, smoother swings require more flexible shafts. Your flex should sync with your natural rhythm and the point where you release the club.

- **Think about your ideal shot shape**. If you hit slices or hooks, a shaft flex that helps straighten your ball flight may improve your game. Talk to a pro about how flex can influence the shot shape.

The shaft is the engine of your clubs, so investing in a proper flex for your swing can make a huge difference in your ball striking and accuracy. Take the time to test out your options and get very fitted for the right shaft flex.

The only way to know for sure if a particular shaft flex is right for you is to:

- Test it out on the golf course.

- Work with your local pro shop to try different flexes in your driver and irons.

- See which shaft flex produces the most solid, consistent strikes, best accuracy, and distance.

Choosing the right shaft can shave strokes off your game. Keep these guidelines in mind and understand that finding your perfect shaft flex needs an experimental period. The time invested will be worth it when stripping the ball down the fairway and sticking it close to the pin. To make an informed decision on your next club purchase, don't get overwhelmed by all the options — start with the fundamentals, get fitted for your shafts, and find what works for your game. You'll strike the ball farther, straighter, and quicker with the right shafts in your golf bag. That new driver with the upgraded shaft is just what you need to finally break 100 or 90.

Chapter 6: Club Maintenance and Care

5. Proper maintenance and care ensure your club maintains its durability and effectiveness. Source: https://www.pexels.com/search/dirty%20golf%20club%20being% 20cleaned/

Owning a golf club is an investment. These items last a lifetime when maintained and stored properly. As a golfer, you'll find replacing one of your clubs quite challenging because you've grown accustomed to them. They've become part of the furniture. You've trained and played many golf games with them many times and have grown your skills with this equipment. You'd probably like to preserve them in a museum if you had your way. Given that it is hard to replace a club that suits you so well, you ought to think of ways to care for and preserve it so that it lasts a long time and remains effective. Proper care ensures your club maintains its durability and effectiveness.

When you clean and regularly run check-ups on your sports gear, you increase the longevity of your clubs. On top of that, you will also ensure no drastic decrease in the resale value.

In this chapter, you're given tips on:

- How to take good care of your clubs
- The right cleaning materials to use
- How best to store your clubs
- How to properly maintain your equipment to ensure longevity
- When to re-grip your clubs if they are ever worn out

The quality of your club and swing affects the trajectory of the ball, so a poorly cared-for club is going to affect your performance. You've spent lots of money on your irons. You don't want to spend more on unnecessary maintenance charges. You can take other cleaning approaches beyond using soap and water. This guide provides you with steps on how to clean your clubs manually.

Why Should You Clean Your Clubs?

Cleaning your clubs extends their life span and gives them a shiny finish. Without regular maintenance, dirt and debris will accumulate, causing your practice to lose balance and fluidity of flight, and won't look good on you or your games.

To undergo an effective cleanup system, use a cleaning kit or have a mixture of water and soap with a soft-bristled brush. Do not keep your clubs in the water for too long, as this will damage them. Using a cleaning kit is a better option, but if you don't have access to one or insist on going manual, here's a guide on how to clean your club:

Step 1

To begin, you can make good use of your dishwashing liquid soap. This first step aims to create as many suds (foam) as possible. When the liquid is at the bottom of the bucket, vigorously squirt until you produce ample foam.

Next, add a measurable amount of warm water. Ensure the water isn't too hot and doesn't completely overshadow the suds. You should never use hot water because the ferrule connecting the club heads doesn't solidify, making it impossible to stick your club's head back into the shafts.

Fill the bucket enough only to cover your hands. Work with warm water until it gets foamy. This cleaning method only works for your club heads, not the shafts or grips.

Step 2

With the first stage complete, it is time to clean your club head. While the water is at a ready temperature (warm), place your club head alone into the water, ensuring that it is completely submerged.

While the club head is in the water, make sure the ferrules are kept above the suds level. Leave the club head in the water for a couple of minutes. Doing this will loosen up any dirt accumulated within your club's grooves during games. The suds also help break those golf course chemicals built into the club's surface.

Carry out this procedure for about 5-10 minutes or longer if you feel your club is extremely dirty.

Step 3

After soaking your club head, softly brush the surface of your club with a bristle brush or a toothbrush. This procedure removes any hidden dirt from the groove's surface. Every part of your club head needs cleaning, especially the sole that touches and rubs the ground before a shoot. This is to prevent rusting and give long-term maintenance.

Do not forget to clean the back of your club head, especially the areas you feel would likely have collected dust. If you find more dirt on the club head, soak it for a few extra minutes. Avoid using wired bristle brushes — these could cause a scratch on the surface.

Your bristle brush must reach into every part of your grooves and wipe any residual dirt off. If this brush is too soft, try using a golf tee or an old toothbrush.

Step 4

Rinse out your club in another bucket of warm water. Make sure that the grooves are fully tended to by using your bristle brush. Lastly, don't let water get into the shaft, as this will cause severe damage to your club.

Step 5

Dry the head of your club with a towel. Wipe the shaft if some water accidentally splashes on it. Drying removes any remaining dirt on your club's surface.

Before placing your club into your golf bag, it needs to be completely dry to avoid dampness seeping into your bag. You can apply a polish product for a final touch, but ensure you have sundried it before removing it. You can then place your club in storage.

Storing Your Club the Right Way

Correctly storing your club is just as important as cleaning it. This might not necessarily cross the mind of many golfers, but as you get into the game, you start to see the benefits of storing equipment properly. If you want to guarantee that your most trusted club has a long life span, use the following storage tips.

1. Choose the Right Storage Location

Your storage location may vary if you are a frequent golf player or one who partakes in seasonal and monthly games. As a frequent player, you've probably considered the trunk of your car as the best storage location for your clubs, but this comes with a downside. The downside is that car trunks become extremely hot when your car is parked in the sun — high temperature breaks the ferrule that joins the club and shaft. Using your garage as a storage location is best to avoid this. This is vital if you're a seasonal or a daily player. Temperature matters for a long-lasting club. Remember you need a completely dry area in your garage for storage. If your garage is humid, store your clubs inside your home.

2. Choose the Right Positioning

Have your clubs positioned correctly in storage. Do not place your clubs at a slant or in a horizontal position. They should be placed appropriately and not touching each other. If this happens, it can lead to dents or scratches to the club head.

3. Use a Good Golf Bag

It can be hard work trying to place your clubs separate from each other and positioned uprightly. If necessary, the best solution for this problem is to use a golf bag. In a golf bag, individual compartments are made for each club. Your clubs will be more organized, eliminating the possibility of one ruining the other. Aside from a golf bag, you can try out a hard-shell casing for transportation and storage. With this, you can be certain that your clubs are extra protected while you move or drive around with them.

4. Use Head Covers for Your Clubs

Head covers give your clubs extra protection against scratches and dents. They shield your clubs from direct sunlight and moisture. Luckily, most golf bags provide extra head covers for your drives and woods. Note, however, that the use of head covers doesn't imply that you can leave your clubs out under the sun or rain. Extreme temperature damages your sporting equipment — so avoid extremely cold or hot areas.

5. Inspect Your Clubs Often

Your clubs are your golf friends, so you should check on them often and ensure they're always in good shape. Set aside time to regularly inspect your clubs — this will save you the heartbreak of seeing a dent or scratch where you can't trace its origin. Regular inspection helps you spot any issues or damage before they get severe. Look out for wear and tear on your club grips, check for scratches or dents, and ensure the shafts are also in good condition. Always avoid hitting your clubs excessively on the ground before taking a shot. If you notice any dents or damage, it's best to take your clubs to a professional repairer.

6. Shaft Care

Prioritizing your club head is essential, but caring for your shafts is equally as important. Take a soft wipe to remove dirt or sweat from your shafts whenever you're out from each round. You also want to avoid leaning or putting much weight on your club shafts because doing that can lead to bending or breaking.

When to Re-grip Your Clubs

Your club grips are not as fragile as your shafts and club heads. They may only need complete changing once or twice a year if your clubs have a long life span — although your club grips might suffer from wear and tear or wear out over time. When worn out, your club grips affect your grip and control over the club.

You know it's time for a re-grip when you notice the following on your club:

- Cracks
- Too smooth or shiny areas
- Loss of thickness

It's recommended to prepare to re-grip your clubs each year between a minimum of 40 to 60 rounds. This may not be the case if you're a seasonal or monthly player. You would have to change your grips only when you notice the aforementioned signs or have nearly played that many rounds. Suppose you're unsure how to read the signs or go about a re-grip. In this case, consult a professional club fitter. Professionals can help you choose the right grips and install them properly.

In addition to that, you should book schedules with a proper club fitter to ensure that your clubs are regularly inspected or fitted. Equipment checks will determine whether your clubs are suitable for your games. A good-fitting club helps you optimize your selection and gives a good shaft flex to enhance your gaming performance. Consider registering at a certified club fitting at least once every few years or whenever you see fit.

Clubs need good maintenance and care to increase their longevity. There are several ways to ensure your clubs get the maintenance they deserve. In this chapter, you've learned how to give your clubs a good clean and how to properly store them to avoid scratches or dents. Remember to hold your club's shafts and grips to the same standard. Avoid extreme hot or cold temperatures, store your clubs in a cool, dry area, and drop them in at a club fitting for a professional check-up to secure their lifespan. Maintaining your clubs can be one tedious task, but it's necessary for their longevity and performance. By following the steps in this chapter, your clubs will be in good condition whenever you need them.

Chapter 7: Enhancing Your Performance with Accessories

Picture this. It's the perfect summer moment on the golf course when the temperature is just right. The sun is gently warming your skin, and there's a light breeze whispering through the trees. Only a few feet remain between the last cup and you, and as you prepare to take your swing, you can't help but wonder if there's the slightest chance of the club slipping away from your hands or your favorite ball getting lost in the vast golf course. Lost in your thoughts, as you strike the ball, you miss your swing just slightly and lose the chance at having your name etched forever in the golfing hall of fame at your local course.

"What's the best way to enhance and elevate your golfing experience?" you ask. The answer is hidden in the world of golfing accessories turning your ordinary day-to-day rounds into extraordinary ones. This chapter delves into various golfing accessories, the unsung heroes equipping you with solid confidence. It'll discuss how a glove that fits you like a second hand and grip enhancers ensure you unlock a new level of accuracy, distance, and consistency.

Why You Should Invest in Quality Golfing Equipment

7.   Investing in quality golfing equipment ensures you unlock a new level of accuracy, distance, and consistency. Source: https://unsplash.com/photos/KwzcJtgVEK8

If you've been around the field for some time and have your swing adjusted, you'll realize quality golfing equipment is crucial to get the perfect swing, but a novice may be quick to disregard its value long-term. Some reasons why you should invest in quality equipment are as follows:

Further and Better

One of the most gratifying experiences on the golfing course is seeing your ball airborne in the direction you hoped, and golfing accessories ensure you achieve just that by aiding your performance.

Your Golf Swing

Many factors, such as clubs, gloves, and shoes, impact your golf swing. Even your age, weight, and health play a significant role in your swing, and you'll notice slight variations every time you're out playing. Golfing accessories help you compensate for these variations by providing a better grip and support, so your golfing experience is consistent and smooth.

Protection and Grip

On days you've been swinging too hard on the golf course, you don't want to end up with blisters, and a quality golfing accessory, such as a glove, will provide you with the necessary protection. It also helps to in compensate when you're forming a grip on the golf club so you can focus your power on swinging.

Comfort

Golf is a comfort sport for many, but it can quickly become a hassle if you're not taking advantage of the necessary golfing accessories. Maybe you've been struggling with a poor swing or finding it troublesome to locate your signed and one-of-a-kind golf ball on the never-ending golf course.

It can be easy to disregard golfing equipment as an option, but when you consider its many benefits, you'll realize they're just as essential as golf clubs and balls. Take a look at this list of golfing accessories and discover how they can enhance your game's experience.

Golf Gloves

What comes next after golf clubs and balls? If you guessed gloves, you're right! Ensure you find a pair of gloves that fit and feel comfortable on your hands. Well-fitted golf gloves create more friction and tackiness between your hand and the golf club. It allows for a better and more precise swing so you can reach a greater distance. Golf gloves are typically worn individually by players on their non-dominant hands, but to prevent chafing, players opting to wear gloves on both hands are not unheard of.

Poorly-fitting gloves will restrict your ability to gain maximum grip and result in an inaccurate swing. Once you find a pair of gloves suited for your hands, stash a few extras and change them as they wear out.

Golf Rangefinder

If you're spending a good ten minutes second-guessing the distance you need to hit the ball before making the swing, a golf rangefinder is the perfect accessory for you. Instead of doing the mental math yourself, this handy gadget will eliminate all the guesswork and efficiently gauge the distance between holes from your current position. Typically, rangefinders work by having you aim its sighting scope on the flag. The calibrated gauge in the optics measures the distance based on the flagstick's height. Newer rangefinders are simpler and operate by simply sighting any target and pressing a switch to read the distance.

Before using one, you should check with your local golf course if a rangefinder is allowed because, according to Rules 14-3 of golfing, it is illegal to use one, especially during tournaments. For recreational golfers, however, rangefinders are acceptable. The portable device can be clipped to your bag or kept in your pocket.

Divot Repair Tool

Also known as the ball mark repair tool, a divot tool repairs a ball mark left after it hits the ground on its approach shot. You'll need to push gently inwards from all sides around the ident to restore the ball mark. Doing so loosens the compacted turf and allows rapid regrowth of grass. The smooth flat bottom of the putter is used to flatten the surface.

Comfortable Shoes and Insoles

It's wise to invest in comfortable and good shoes and insoles for all-day comfort on the green. A round can last several hours, and whether you're walking or riding around in a cart, you'll be spending a ton of time on your feet. Golfers wear special shoes, which can either be spike-less or have spikes attached to the soles. You can opt for plastic or metal spikes but remember that golf courses often ban metal spikes and only allow plastic spikes during play. The spikes penetrate the grass and soil to help players keep their balance during the swing and increase traction. Shoes can make or break your game, and you'll need to invest in a good pair to minimize the fatigue and ache your feet will experience after spending a long day on the green.

Stroke Counters

You may keep track of how many strokes you make during a hole with the use of a stroke counter. It can be an entire round or a single play. The simplest consist of clickers, beads, and thumbwheels. Each time you make a stroke, you'll record it on your scorecard and go on to the next hole. However, you can get a descriptive graph of your performance throughout the course of your game from newer versions, which also offer varying degrees of power, the ability to track multiple holes and total scores, and more.

Lead Tape

Lead tape consists of a thin strip of adhesive-backed lead and is used by golfers to add weight to specific areas of their golf clubs. The strategic placement of lead tape on the club head allows you to manipulate the club's swing weight. It refers to the weight and balance of the club you feel during the swing, and if you prefer having a heavier club head feel, you can add lead tape to provide more control and stability during the swing.

Ball Retrievers

These are telescoping poles that have a device at the end designed to scoop and trap golf balls. They're used to reclaim balls from water hazards and are often banned during tournaments. Ensure you check the local rules before using one.

Padded Straps

Walking the course with a bag loaded with equipment is a sport on its own, and to make it as relaxing as possible, you'll need a bag with reliable, padded straps. It allows an even distribution of the weight across your shoulders and reduces back and spinal pains. Travel bags come with various features, along with padded straps. These include zippers and bag covers protecting your equipment from abuse and theft.

Golf Umbrella

It's difficult to focus on your game when you're soaked, and on days your friendly weather reporter says it'll rain, taking an umbrella with you to the course is worth it. Invest in a good quality and lightweight umbrella. Make sure it's wide to cover the area required when you make the swing.

Golf Headcovers

Even though the newer versions of golf clubs are made of strong metal alloys and are capable of withstanding more than traditional wooden clubs, they're still susceptible to damage when in transit or use. When you walk or ride the course, the heads and shafts of clubs move around and come into contact with one another. The jostling can create nicks and dents in your clubs, devaluing them and lowering their longevity. Invest in good quality golf head covers, and ensure they come with padded protection.

Brushes

If you've got a favorite golf ball, consider investing in a good brush. They feature handles and bristles designed to clean debris from various parts of the golf clubs and balls without leaving any marks on them. The primary purpose of using a golf brush is to maintain your equipment and increase its longevity. Regularly cleaning your equipment ensures maximum functionality and enhances your overall golfing experience. Cleaner cubs offer better contact with the ball, allowing greater accuracy and control of your swings. A clean ball can easily glide through the air, and without the added weight of debris, it'll guarantee a consistent flight.

Towels

Golf bags come with a ring or a hook, which can be used to tie or clip a golf towel. An obvious use of the towel is to wipe off sweat, but it can also be used to clean and dry balls and club faces. There are towels designed specifically for golf courses and players. For cleaning clubs and balls, pieces of the towel are made of rougher materials and fastened to it with a carabiner or clip. The softer sections can be used to dry your equipment without scratching it.

Golf accessories can enhance your performance whether you're a beginner or an expert. Now that you're aware of the various types of golfing accessories and aids, consider experimenting with them and figuring out what works best for you.

Chapter 8: Tips for Improving Your Golf Game

8. *Golf is a game of precision, strategy, and continuous growth, which you can only improve at with practice. Source: https://unsplash.com/photos/mqPSdQDWeM8*

Whether it's a hobby or a competitive sport, you only get good at it by continually practicing and improving. This chapter will guide you on improving at golf, a game of precision, strategy, and continuous growth. You'll learn how to command and develop a consistent swing, master club selection for different shots, and explore pitfalls novice players encounter that hinder their progress.

But that's not all — you'll also explore the mental game and course management of golfing. You'll learn to harness the power of your mind and make decisions such as how hard to hit the ball and in what direction to swing, considering the wind direction that particular day. Take a look at how you can improve your golf game.

Developing a Consistent Swing

If you've been shooting 79 one day and 90 the next, it's time to look at your golf swing. A perfect swing requires harmony, and your whole body must be in sync to deliver a powerful strike. You'll learn to use your body weight and movement to your advantage with some practice. Learn how you can develop a consistent swing throughout your golfing games with these tips.

Establish a Strong Pre-Shot Routine

A pre-shot routine is a systematic procedure players establish to hit consistent golf goals. It includes a sequence of movements and thoughts a golfer executes before making the swing. It's one of the most acknowledged yet underused techniques established by golfers, and to hit consistent golf shots, you'll need to develop a pre-shot routine. The following are parts of a typical pre-shot routine, and you'll learn how to customize each to your advantage.

Stop and Think

The stage starts once you approach the ball. Take some time and observe the distance to the target, the wind direction, the way the ball faces, and your club selection.

Preparation is key, and the more you're aware of your immediate environment, the better chance you'll have at delivering a strong swing.

Prepare and Rehearse

Before making the swing, practice delivering the shot you intend to play. During the practice swing, address your position, aim your club face, and align your feet and body accordingly. A practice swing will help you predict the momentum and force required to hit the ball a certain distance.

Execute Your Shot

At this point, novice players often freeze, and to help you power through it, consider practicing a positive mental mantra. It can be a power pose or a quote from your favorite book or movie. While keeping the position you practiced, initiate and execute the swing.

Take Your Time

Don't rush through the process, and take your time planning the shot. During tournaments, players have between 50 seconds to 1 minute to play their shot and fit their pre-shot process within this timeframe. As a beginner, take as long as you need. Once you've established a routine, follow through with it in under one minute.

Choose a Grip and Stick To It

The grip is an intermediary between you and the golf club. If your hands are in an uncomfortable position, it will impact your performance negatively. Problems with the grip will cause inconsistency in your golf swings, and to ensure it doesn't happen, you'll need unwavering confidence when standing in the address position. Below is the 5-step procedure to maximize your natural potential and guarantee a more consistent ball flight.

Start with Your Lead Hand

A good grip will improve the individual natural motion that each player has. Your lead hand should first be on the handle in its natural position. Standing straight and letting your arms hang freely will help you locate the position if you're having problems. Avoid holding a ball or adopting a golf stance. Once completely relaxed, grip a club, which will be your starting point. It won't require any manipulation, and you'll be able to start and finish your swing.

Fine Tune Your Posture

Even if you've identified your natural posture, it'll require some fine-tuning before moving ahead. Double-check that your lead-hand grip and lead-hip mobility match. If the two aren't in sync, you'll deliver inconsistent shots. As you hold the club in your address stance with your trail hand on the handle, put your weight on the front side with your hands forward and your hips as open as you can.

Position Your Trail Hand

Hold your club out front at a 45-degree angle. Place your trial hand and ensure you do it through the base of your fingers and not your palm. It'll let your fingers wrap the handle easily, providing a better grip. Hold the handle in your trail hand like you're used to holding a suitcase when in doubt.

Practice the Cast Drill

Throw the club forward as if throwing a fishing line by bringing it over your trail shoulder while holding the grip in both hands. It helps mimic the trail arm extension, which takes place in all downswings. While practicing the cast swing, observe if a certain position limits your swing's potential. Keep adjusting until you're able to maximize your swing's impact.

Practice with Alignment Sticks

Golf alignment sticks are long, thin, and flexible rods used by golfers to help align their bodies and clubs to the target. Golf beginners often utilize them in practice. It aids in the swing path, stops swaying, and helps keep your head still. Here's how you can use golf alignment sticks to your benefit.

Check Your Alignment

Correct alignment is critical in golfing, and an inconsistent aim can easily ruin a good game. Using golf alignment sticks in your routine can help you understand and bridge the gap between your perceived and actual aim.

Check Ball Position

A golf swing's most overlooked element is the ball position. Often golfers attribute their miss-hits to a poor golf swing. However, you'll observe it's due to the ball position being out of place. Alignment sticks help position your ball correctly, ensuring you get the perfect swing and hit.

Mastering Club Selection for Different Shots

Whether you carry a complete set of 14 golf clubs, or a starter set, you've got to know which club to hit from whenever your ball lands closer to the hole. Considering the infinite combination of distance, weather, and other factors can be challenging, but it will soon become second nature with practice.

You need to consider two inputs when determining the club for your next shot. The distance between you and the target and how far you'll typically hit the club. Estimating the correct distance takes time and experience but consider driving a range to understand what a certain number of yards feel like. Most have markers at specific numbers, such as 25, 50, 75, and 100 yards. The following steps will help you gauge a better estimate:

- Pick your shortest club, and aim for the nearest target.

- Ensure you hit the shot with power and relatively straight. After it lands, estimate how far it's from the closest target. The distance the ball traveled in the air should only be estimated; the roll the ball experienced after landing shouldn't be included.

- Once you've taken three measurements, average them out to get the yardage for that specific club.

Golfers typically notice a 10 to 15 yard difference when switching from one club to another.

Once you're done with the above exercise, note down the average yardage for each club on your phone or a piece of paper. You can refer to them when you're on the green next time, and soon you'll know them all by heart. Remember that as your swing gets better, you'll hit the ball further and may overestimate the power required for a certain shot, causing your ball to fly past the target. Adjust your ball yardages with time to accommodate the changes.

Common Mistakes to Avoid as a Beginner

1. Not Choosing the Right Golf Clubs

It's easy to fall into the trap of fancy equipment, but you don't have to go out and buy a custom set of clubs before you've even started golfing regularly. A cheap set will help you get started, and if you miss the ball and strike the ground, a new set won't break your bank.

2. Neglecting to Warm-up

Golf may not be as fast-paced as other sports, but it requires strenuous muscle activity. Swinging the golf club around without a quick pre-game warm-up will do a number on your muscles and may lead to injuries. Beginners often suffer from pulled muscles on their first few swings of the day. To prevent bodily harm, do a few gentle practice swings before hitting the ball to activate and warm up your muscles.

3. Only Practicing Your Drivers

Don't get stuck on practicing the long shots every time you step out on the green. It's equally crucial to ensure you get the hang of chips, medium-range shots, and putts if you hope to become a competent player. Practice the wide variety of shots each time you're on the golf field.

4. Giving Up

Golfing may seem a simple sport on the surface, but once you start practicing it religiously, you'll realize many dynamics are at play. Beginners hang up their clubs and never touch the sport again after messing up too many times. Like with any other sport, you'll struggle, but it doesn't mean you should get frustrated and quit. Be willing to learn, revise the strategies outlined in this book, and believe in yourself.

Throughout this chapter, you've explored how to improve your golf game and learned the nuances of developing a consistent swing, selecting the right clubs, and avoiding common mistakes. Armed with this newfound knowledge, it's time you embark on a journey toward improving and enhancing your golfing experience.

Conclusion

Golf is certainly not the easiest of games with its many rules and principles, and in this book, you've gone over the major component – the golf club. There are many things to learn about golf clubs and how the various types are designed to suit different occasions on the course, and without a proper guide, it will be impossible to get a handle on them. This comprehensive book on mastering golf clubs for beginners has equipped you with the essential knowledge and skills to understand, select, and utilize your golf clubs for maximum peak performance. Each chapter has broadened your knowledge of this prized tool, from the basics to advanced tips on improving your game. The range of topics — drivers and woods, irons and hybrids, wedges and specialty clubs, understanding shaft types and flex, club maintenance and care, enhancing your performance with accessories, and finally, invaluable tips for taking your golf game to the next level — were written to provide all golf enthusiasts with a solid foundation. With these core foundations, you'll see that golf is more than just a game. Hopefully, your passion for this sport will spur you to commit to it.

As a beginner venturing into the world of golf, armed with the knowledge from this book, you will be able to take to the course and put your newfound skills into practice. Remember to approach each swing with confidence and embrace the joy of the game.

Before you go, you could take a moment to leave a review on "Golf Clubs for Beginners." Your feedback is invaluable and will help continue to improve and provide even better resources for aspiring golfers like yourself. Your review will also assist other readers in making an informed decision about this book.

Thank you for joining this golfing journey, and good luck with many more enjoyable rounds of golf ahead. May your clubs always bring you closer to achieving your best performance on the course!

References

(N.d.). Dickssportinggoods.com. https://www.dickssportinggoods.com/protips/sports-and-activities/golf/how-to-buy-a-golf-driver#:~:text=Drivers%20are%20commonly%20used%20on,golfers%20at%20every%20level%20need.

A 6-step plan to grip the golf club better than ever. (2022, March 26). Golf. https://golf.com/instruction/6-step-plan-grip-better-than-ever/

Barwald, C. (n.d.). Which golf clubs should you have in your bag: A quick guide to ensure you're carrying the right equipment for your game. Minutegolf - Online Golf Reservations. https://www.minutegolf.ca/index.php?option=com_content&view=article&id=121:which-golf-clubs-should-you-have-in-your-bag&catid=9&lang=en&Itemid=153

Beginner golf tip: How to choose the correct club for a shot. (2013, April 11). Golf-info-guide.com. https://golf-info-guide.com/golf-tips/beginner-golf-tips/beginner-golf-tip-how-to-choose-the-correct-club-for-a-shot/

Del Sol, C. (n.d.). Hybrid golf clubs: when to use them. Visitacostadelsol.com. https://blog.visitacostadelsol.com/en/hybrid-golf-clubs

Drivers – Golf Term. (2011, September 16). Golf-info-guide.com. https://golf-info-guide.com/golf-terms/driver-the-driver-or-no-1-wood/

Foxwell, T. (2020, August 24). The importance of quality golfing equipment. ADAPT Network. https://www.adaptnetwork.com/sports/golf/how-quality-golf-equipment-can-improve-your-game/

Golf club parts - illustrated definitions of golf terms. (2018, February 21). Golf Distillery. https://www.golfdistillery.com/definitions/club-parts/

Golf clubs – what are drivers, woods, irons & wedges? (n.d.). Mytimeactive.co.uk. https://www.mytimeactive.co.uk/wellbeing-mission/golf-clubs-what-are-drivers-woods-irons-wedges

Golf wedges explained: Understand your short-game golf clubs. (2023, February 4). GoGolf365. https://gogolf365.com/blogs/news/golf-wedges-explained-understand-your-short-game-golf-clubs

Golf, D. (2022, June 22). Golf shafts: An introduction to the types of shafts. Deemples Golf. https://deemples.com/blog/golf-shafts-an-introduction-to-the-types-of-shafts

Hogan, B. (n.d.). What are the different types of golf irons? Bestgolfaccessories.net. https://bestgolfaccessories.net/blog/what-are-the-different-types-of-golf-irons/

Hogg, J. (2022, December 22). How to choose golf irons. Golf Monthly Magazine; Golf Monthly. https://www.golfmonthly.com/gear/how-to-choose-golf-irons

How to pick the right golf shaft. (2019a, October 15). Golfsupport Blog; Golfsupport. https://golfsupport.com/blog/how-to-pick-the-right-golf-shaft/

How to store golf clubs properly. (n.d.). Hjgt.org. https://www.hjgt.org/news/how-to-store-golf-clubs-properly

Jooste, C. (2020, January 20). How to clean golf clubs and make them last longer. Golf Span – Golf Tips and Equipment Reviews. https://www.golfspan.com/how-to-clean-golf-clubs

Kelley, B. (2004, March 15). Types of golf clubs: The complete guide. TripSavvy. https://www.tripsavvy.com/meet-the-golf-clubs-1560507

Kelley, B. (2008, July 21). Bump and run golf shot (definition). LiveAbout. https://www.liveabout.com/bump-and-run-1564086

KunLehane. (2021, March 26). Pros And Cons Of Hybrid Golf Clubs – the ultimate golfing resource. The Expert Golf Website. https://southamptongolfclub.com/pros-and-cons-of-hybrid-golf-clubs/

Lashen, W. (2018, May 28). The truth about golf shafts that every golfer should know. Pete's Golf. https://www.petesgolf.com/golf-shafts/

Lesson #1: The basics of golf clubs. (n.d.).
Pinemeadowgolf.com.
https://www.pinemeadowgolf.com/golf-clubs-101/1-basics

Mahfuz, R. (2023, April 8). How long to wait after re-
gripping golf clubs? Golf Reply. https://golfreply.com/how-
long-to-wait-after-regripping-golf-clubs/

Must-have golf accessories. (2021, May 28). VESSEL.
https://vesselgolf.com/blogs/blog/must-have-golf-
accessories

Olizarowicz, B. (2022, August 5). 10 proven tips to get more
consistency in your golf swing. Golf Workout Program.
https://golfworkoutprogram.com/golf-swing-consistency/

Rookie Road. (2020, August 13). What is Bump and Run in
Golf? Rookieroad.com; Rookie Road.
https://www.rookieroad.com/golf/what-is-bump-and-run/

Shaw, G. (2022, February 22). Golf pre-shot routine:
Everything you need to know. Golf Monthly Magazine; Golf
Monthly. https://www.golfmonthly.com/tips/golf-pre-shot-
routine-everything-you-need-to-know

The pitching wedge: Set wedge vs. Specialty wedge - the golf
performance center. (2021, January 22). The Golf
Performance Center - The Northeast's Premier Junior Golf
Academy. https://thegolfperformancecenter.com/5-
elements-blog/equipment/the-pitching-wedge-match-the-
iron-set-or-specialty-wedge/

Types of golf clubs - illustrated guide into golf club types.
(2018, February 21). Golf Distillery.
https://www.golfdistillery.com/definitions/clubs/

Valentin, B. (n.d.). 7 common golfing mistakes to avoid for beginners. Northlandcountryclub.com. https://www.northlandcountryclub.com/blog/56-common-golfing-mistakes-to-avoid-for-beginners

Waddington, J. (2022, December 28). Types of golf irons (defining what's right for you). Golf Educate. https://golfeducate.com/what-are-the-different-types-of-golf-irons/

Wallace, C. (2015, January 12). Club Fitting 101: Why you should get fit and what you need to know. Golf Advisor. https://www.golfpass.com/travel-advisor/articles/club-fitting-101-why-you-should-get-fit-and-what-you-need-to-know

What to consider when shopping for golf shafts for drivers. (n.d.). Dallas Golf Company. https://www.dallasgolf.com/blogwhat-to-consider-when-shopping-for-golf-shafts-for-drivers/

WhysGuy, W. (2023, February 6). How to use golf alignment sticks. WhyGolf. https://whygolf.com/blogs/whysguyscorner/how-to-use-golf-alignment-sticks

Wood - golf club type - illustrated definition & guide. (2018, February 21). Golf Distillery. https://www.golfdistillery.com/definitions/clubs/woods

Printed in Great Britain
by Amazon